Bootstrap Words
(Pull Yourself Up!)

Bootstrap Words
(Pull Yourself Up!)
Second Edition

Maura Beatty

KENDALL/HUNT PUBLISHING COMPANY
4050 Westmark Drive   Dubuque, Iowa 52002

Published by Kendall/Hunt Publishing Company.

Copyright © 1995, 1996 by Maura Beatty

All rights reserved. No part of this book may be reproduced or transmitted in any form or by any means, electronic or mechanical, including photocopying, recording or by any information storage or retrieval system without written permission from the author, except for the inclusion of brief quotations in a review.

Library of Congress Catalog Card Number: 95-82344

ISBN: 0-7872-1982-7

Page 43: From *Illusions: The Adventures of a Reluctant Messiah* by Richard Bach. Copyright © 1977 by Richard Bach and Leslie Parrish-Bach. Used by permission of Delacorte Press, a division of Bantam Doubleday Dell Publishing Group, Inc.

Cover Design by Chuck Beatty

Back Cover Photo by Greer Evans

Book Design by Maura and Chuck Beatty

For Chuck Beatty,
the string to my balloon…

Table of Contents

Preface	ix
Acknowledgments	xi
The Bootstrap Words	1

Part One (1968–1986)   Glimmers of Light in the Dark   3
In which I had a lot to learn.

Part Two (1986–1989)   A Brighter Light in a Bigger Dark   23
In which I was trying to trust the process.

Part Three (1990–1994)   The Light Surrounds Me, the Darkness Recedes   39
In which I used affirmations as the springboard to my future.

Part Four (1987–1995)   Spreading the Light   69
In which I have the privilege of sharing with others.

Epilogue	95
Index	97

Preface

Bootstrap Words is the story of a journey.

If you look up the word *bootstrap*, you will find the definition that inspired the title of this book:

> **bootstrap** *tr.v.* To promote and develop by use of one's own initiative and work without reliance on outside help. —***Idiom. by one's own bootstraps.*** By one's own efforts.
>
> The American Heritage Dictionary, 3rd Edition

You may wonder how I can title a book that celebrates the influence of others with a word that means reliance on oneself. I believe that there is a difference between being motivated, supported and encouraged by others, and depending on yourself to take action. When it comes right down to it, you're the only one who can start the ball rolling. The words in this book were my bootstraps; I used them to pull *myself* up.

This book is composed of four sections, each with its own focus.

Part One is about my earliest introduction to positive thoughts. There are relatively few quotes covering a long span of time. During this period, I was dealing with overwhelming emotion on a daily basis. Positive thinking was not high on my list of priorities. I had a lot to learn.

Part Two is about facing a specific challenge, and using what I had learned to deal with it. By this time, I had seen some encouraging results when I tested my capacity for positive thought. I was trying to trust the process.

Part Three is about what happened when I took a leap of faith. Not only did I believe that using positive affirmations would change my life, I counted on that belief to be the springboard to my future!

Part Four is the result of the work I did along the way. Not only was I using positive motivation every day, I was actually thinking positively! The way I had learned to look at life and interact with people had completely changed me. And I was given, through my work, the privilege of sharing my thoughts with others.

It is my hope that this book will motivate you to look at life more positively, to find your own spirit and celebrate it. I have discovered that it is both the challenges and the triumphs that make our travels unique. I hope you'll find something in the pages that follow that will feed your heart as you make your own way.

It is an honor to share the journey with you.

Maura Beatty
Austin, Texas
October 1995

Acknowledgments

None of us succeeds alone. The support of others is always the celebration of our glory. It is my privilege to thank the following people for their support with this project:

My parents: Dr. D.A. Drennen and M. Eileen Connolly Drennen, who, with all their love, provided me with just what I needed to develop the *fire in the belly* that my work requires.

My sisters and brother: Deirdre, Susan, Eileen, Don and Maribeth, who love me, who continue to teach me what I need to learn and who make me proud to be their sister.

My grandparents: John P. and Helen Reid Connolly, both long passed to their reward, whose love lights my way to this day.

My teachers and champions: Sr. Marie Redempta, Mrs. Beaudette, Sister Mary Agathine, Sister Mary Monica, Kenneth Michael Baron, John & Mary Baron, Father Timone, Brother Simeon, Joe Luna, Mathilde Goldwitz, Dennis C. Kinlaw, the YN2 Yeoman WAVE at CINCLANTFLT, David Michael Martin, George Earl Gochenaur, Jim Mitchell, Jimmie Webb, Dan Adams, Sue MacKenzie and Steve Yerian. Each one of them saw my potential and nurtured it.

My counselors: Gwen Nichols and Mary Lou Holt who taught me that I had wings and showed me how to fly.

The writers, speakers poets and visionaries: Leo Buscaglia, Arthur Conan Doyle, Joseph Campbell, Georgia O'Keefe, Loren Eisley, Tony Hillerman, Marion Zimmer Bradley, Bill W., A. A. Milne, the authors of the quotes in this book, and all the others who share their own thoughts and dreams as lights along the way.

My friends and mentors: The late Joan Compton, whose dignity in dying profoundly affected my desire to live each day to the fullest; David Cleland, who brought me to Texas so I could be in the right place at the right time; the late John Wilson, Professor of Communications, who taught me how important it is to touch the hearts of my audience.

The Beatty Family: Maggie and Al, who had the brilliant idea of bringing Chuck into the world and whose love and generosity to me is a treasured gift; Scott and Beth, our ardent supporters and Mexican supper surprisers, who turn their home into our personal 4-Star Bed & Breakfast at a moments notice; and my new Canadian cousins, who welcomed me into their homes and hearths as if I were returning, not a stranger.

My audiences, clients, fans, friends and colleagues, and everyone who chooses this book: You make the journey worthwhile and the story worth telling.

Finally, three people whose influence on my life has changed me forever:

Deirdre Marie, my sister, true friend and kindred spirit: You've been with me since the beginning. If you hadn't come into this life as my sister, we'd have found each other as friends. You are a treasure in my life, always.

Maggie, the best friend I ever had: You loved me on sight. You stood up for me, challenged me, and grew with me through all the adventures of these past 12 years. You taught me unconditional love. I cherish you, always.

Chuck, the true love of my soul: You paint the days of my life in the most glorious of colors and the tenderest of hues. You are the wind beneath my wings and the apple of my eye. I love you, always.

Thank you!

Bootstrap Words
(Pull Yourself Up!)

Although the person I am today is a joyful and grateful woman, I have not always been this way.

The seeds of joy and gratitude were always there—buried beneath the surface. In the pain of my growing up, they simply had no chance to flourish.

By the time I ran away from home at age seventeen, I was arrogant and angry. I had a long way to go to find happiness.

As I moved toward my destiny, the words in this section provided the...

...Glimmers of Light in the Dark

Part One: 1968–1985

When I was a sophomore at Our Lady of Lourdes High School in Poughkeepsie, New York, one of my teachers was Father Timone. He introduced us to Teilhard de Chardin, who was buried nearby at what was then St. Andrews-on-the-Hudson; now the Culinary Institute of America.

Father Timone was a significant friend to me. Several years later, when I found this quote in a magazine, I cut it out and pasted it in my diary. When I look at it, I remember him and smile. I was always searching for the Energy of Love.

"Someday, after we have mastered the winds, the waves, the tides and gravity, we shall harness for God the Energies of Love. Then, for the second time in the history of the world, Man will have discovered fire."

– Teilhard De Chardin

I've had this quote from the time I was in high school. It may be that my mother gave it to me, but I can't be sure.

Whether she did or not, it always reminds me of her. It represented the way I believed she felt about me.

It reminded me of how I wanted to be and what kind of love I wanted to have in my life—although it would take me many years to find it.

"There is no difficulty that enough love will not conquer; no disease that enough love will not heal. No door that enough love will not open; no gulf that enough love will not bridge. No wall that enough love will not throw down, and no sin that enough love will not redeem. It makes no difference how deeply seated the trouble; how hopeless the outlook; how muddled the tangle; how great the mistake. A sufficient realization will dissolve it all."

—Unknown

Every time I read this quote, I travel back to 1978 and see myself sitting on the floor of my two-room apartment in San Diego. I found this quote in a magazine and tore it out to save.

I had just completed a three year enlistment in the U. S. Navy, sandblasting and painting submarines. I was trying to figure out what to do with my life.

This quote was like a flash of light for me—intriguing in its possibilities. At the time, I did not know why these words touched me so deeply.

Today I know. And I still have that magazine page.

> "We Know What We Are, But Not What We May Be."
>
> —William Shakespeare

This is another quote from that same time in San Diego. I was about 26, living on my six months of unemployment from the Navy. For the first time in my life, I was taking the opportunity to just breathe and relax. I was running two to three miles a day and learning yoga.

It seemed like I had my whole life ahead of me, and I had no idea what to do with it. I was certainly doing a lot of thinking.

These words intrigued me, although I couldn't put my finger on why.

"To *Know* is Nothing at All. To *Imagine* is Everything."

—ANATOLE FRANCE

Celebrating was a new idea to me when I first found this quote. "Celebrate" seemed like such an overpowering idea. It was bigger than "party" and seemed to suggest a joy I had never felt. I wanted to feel it, though.

At the time, my heart was too full of pain for me to consider what it might be like to feel it "being right."

Even so, when I first read these words, they struck a chord in my heart. And, although I had no idea what they meant, my heart must have sensed the possibilities. This quote has been up on the wall of every place I have lived since 1978.

"Celebrate the
Doing Right
and Being Right
of Your Heart"

—RAINIER MARIA RILKE

My friend Carol was a kindred soul—another searcher. We met on a bus travelling from downtown San Diego to Ocean Beach.

Neither of us had the courage to speak to the other until we met again at a continuing education class. We became fast friends after that. The glue that held our friendship together was our search for the answers to the question of our purpose in life.

She sent me this poem, written in pencil on a sheet of notebook paper. I still have it, though I've long since lost track of her. I hope she found her answers. This poem contained one of mine.

"*Unanswered Yet?* Faith cannot be unanswered…Unanswered yet? Nay, do not say ungranted. Perhaps your part is not wholly done. The work began when your first prayer was uttered, and God will finish what He has begun. If you will keep the incense burning true, this glory you shall see, sometime, somewhere."

—Robert Browning

One of my favorite places in San Diego was the health food co-op in Ocean Beach. It smelled wonderful in there—herbs and incense and fresh food all blending into one heavenly aroma.

It was a feast for the eyes, as well—full of books and posters, calendars and cards, all painted in the most joyous colors.

This quote is from a poster I bought there. I hung it on my wall as a testament to my belief that this kind of life was possible.

I'm not sure when I lost—or gave away—that poster. I recently found the text written in my journal from 1981. In my life today, I've found the truth of the sentiment.

"To laugh often and love much; to win the respect of children; to earn the approbation of honest critics and endure the betrayal of false friends; to appreciate beauty; to find the best in others; to give of oneself; to leave the world a bit better, whether by a healthy child, a garden patch, or a redeemed social condition; to have played and laughed with enthusiasm and sung with exultation; to know even one life has breathed easier because you have lived—this is to have succeeded."

—RALPH WALDO EMERSON

My sister Deirdre epitomizes this quote for me. In 1982 she sent me a handmade Valentine—this written out and a small red heart pasted to it. Her tenderness speaks volumes about the kind of person she is.

As children, we all used to watch the Wizard of Oz *as a special treat. The six of us would pile into the TV room—all bathed and shampooed, in our pajamas, ready for school the next day.*

One of my favorite characters was the Tin Man. I identified the most with his line, "Now I know *I have a heart, because it's breaking." I spent a lot of years feeling exactly that way.*

Deirdre's card was a reminder of the power of love—the one thing that mends broken hearts.

"Remember, my sentimental friend, that a heart is not judged by how much you love, but by how much you are loved by others."

—THE WIZARD OF OZ

By 1985, I had reenlisted in the Navy and had served 6 more years. I was stationed in Jacksonville, Florida, as a substance abuse counselor.

I was miserable. I wanted to be back in Texas with my husband and my friends. As a brand new counselor, my biggest challenge was taking care of myself.

My first day on the job, I noticed this quote on a plaque on the wall. These words were the catalyst that motivated me to take action to change my circumstances. Getting home a year early was only one of the positive outcomes.

In 1986, I met a woman who was selling a goal-setting program. When I saw this quote on the cover, I knew I had to know the rest of the story!

"That Which You Can Conceive Of, Believe In and Confidently Expect, Must Necessarily Become Your Experience."

—Paul J. Meyer

By 1986, I had accomplished more than I had ever believed possible. Every day, I was making a conscious effort to use the skills I had learned in training and therapy to make positive choices.

By the end of 1989, I had survived a non-stop struggle for sanity and survival. My positive choices had challenged every one of my relationships. My entire world turned upside-down. It seemed as if choosing myself *meant that I had to let go of—or release in some way—every relationship I cared about. While several people chose to grow with me, most did not.*

My struggle for an expanded self resulted in…

...A Brighter Light in a Bigger Dark

Part Two: 1986–1989

The way I began to make the transition from the Navy to civilian life was by attending public seminars. The more seminars I attended, the more I began to believe that I could actually become a speaker myself.

One of the first steps I took in pursuing this idea was to attend a seminar on public speaking. I gained a lot of confidence there, and I met the late Barney O'Lavin.

He could have been my grandfather. As I started speaking to luncheons and club meetings around town, he'd attend whenever he could. He would always have a camera and a tape recorder and he would give me feedback on my presentation, starting with what he thought I did well.

Like a leprechaun, he'd appear unexpectedly at a program. Then I wouldn't see him for months. Just when I'd start to wonder where he was, he would come to see me again. Barney was always positive, always smiling. He lived this quote from his business card.

I've tried to heed his advice.

"Keep your heart free from hate,
Your mind free from worry.
Live simply, expect little, give much.
Fill your life with love. Scatter sunshine.
Think of others. Do as you would be done by.
Try this for one week,
You'll be surprised by your Good Luck."

—Barney O'Lavin

This is from another poster that inspired me. As I continued to take steps in the new direction I'd chosen for myself, I began to notice positive messages all around me.

By 1987, after spending a total of $11\frac{1}{2}$ years in the Navy, I had developed enough faith in myself and my abilities to get out. My new life included working as a drug and alcohol counselor in a large hospital.

Although the transition involved more changes than I'd bargained for, words like these were helpful in keeping me centered.

Today:

"Mend a quarrel. Seek out a forgotten friend. Write a love letter. Share some treasure. Give a soft answer. Encourage youth. Keep a promise. Find the time. Forgive an enemy. Listen. Apologize if you were wrong. Think first of someone else. Be kind and gentle. Laugh a little. Laugh a little more. Express your gratitude. Gladden the heart of a child. Take pleasure in the beauty and wonder of the earth. Speak your love. Speak it again. Speak it yet again."

—A<small>NONYMOUS</small>

This quote was the last thing I put on the final page of the handout from one of my first stress management classes. Who knows where I found it.

When I was asked to put this program together in September, 1987, I had been a civilian for 30 days. My marriage was in trouble, my mother-in-law was dying of cancer, and I was pretending that I knew what I was doing at my new job. My stress level was off the charts!

For some reason, I paid attention to the positive message in this quote. The stress management program I created contained a checklist of the skills I was using to keep me going. Presenting that program, inspired by this quote, started me on the road to where I am today.

"Nothing splendid has ever been achieved except by those who dared believe that something deep inside of them was far superior to circumstance."

—Bruce Barton

Maggie is my Best Friend In The Whole World. Since we met in 1982, we have mirrored each other so well that we have constantly helped each other grow.

There is no doubt in my mind that my friendship with her has provided me with the building blocks for the positive relationships I have today.

During the period from 1986 to 1989, both of us were struggling. We each had difficult decisions to make. We supported each other, no matter what anyone else said or did.

Her reminders to me about the process of love—that the journey is bigger than present experience—kept me going when circumstances seemed insurmountable.

"Love is a Process."

—Maggie

By December of 1988, I'd finally made the decision to leave my husband, David, and begin the process of divorce. We had been together for eight years. I loved him more than I had ever loved anyone in my life.

It was not enough.

I could not stay in the relationship and continue to grow. And I could not force him to grow with me.

Making that break was the hardest thing I had ever done in my life. What I didn't know, then, was that I had taken the first major step in the process of reclaiming myself.

For the first several months, I read this quote daily—through my tears.

"Your Pain is the Breaking of the Shell that Encloses Your Understanding."

—Kahlil Gibran

In 1981, I was introduced to the concept of the 12-Step Program. The Serenity Prayer was a part of the opening of every meeting. As many times as I recited it, it was years before I had any real understanding of what it meant to me.

By early 1989, the prayer accurately described the manner in which I had chosen to live my life. Once I believed that I possessed the courage to change my own behavior and attitudes, it was much easier to accept the things over which I had no control. Those uncontrollables were often other people's behaviors and attitudes.

My grief over the ending of my marriage was eased as I said this daily—my way.

"I *accept* the serenity to accept the things I cannot change, the courage to change the things I can, and the wisdom to know the difference."

—Maura's version of *The Serenity Prayer*

There were many days during those first months of 1989 when I could do little more than drag myself out of bed, get to school, get to work, return home and sob my heart out. Even though I believed that I was doing what was best for me, the pain I experienced was overwhelming.

I often felt as though I had passed through a mysterious doorway where nothing was familiar but the pain. I could not imagine where all of this agony would lead me. What I did know was that I could not go back to living the way I had been living before I left.

This quote helped me to believe that there was a purpose for the process.

"Your pain is the bitter potion by which the physician within you heals your sick self. Therefore trust the physician and drink his remedy in silence and tranquility; for his hand, though heavy and hard, is guided by the tender hand of the Unseen, and the cup he brings, though it burns your lips, has been fashioned of the clay which the Potter has moistened with His own sacred tears."

—Kahlil Gibran

The quotes I had saved over the years were motivating! By reading and believing, I had succeeded in making changes in my life.

By August of 1989, I had earned my college degree (at age 37!) and was promoted to Counseling Center Director. On December 19th, I met Chuck Beatty when he hired me to present **Stress Busters** at the company where he worked. I soon found out that doing what I loved most in the world had brought me to the doorstep of the man with whom I would share my life. After all the years of doubt, I finally believed I could succeed in life. More than that, I knew that I was capable of loving someone and of accepting love in return.

On March 20, 1990, with Chuck's loving support and our belief in my potential, I left my job to start my own company. This was the first step in my journey as a professional speaker. Believing those "Bootstrap Words" gave me the motivation to live my dream.

And in the process…

*...The Light Surrounds Me,
the Darkness Recedes.*

Part Three: 1990-1994

The dictionary has always been one of my favorite books; I usually own one—or several! When you look in a dictionary, you can find the meaning of things you don't understand. For me, that has always been a comfort.

Perspective was the one thing I felt I lacked when I started my company. Looking up the word gave me some relief. I knew that I would gain more perspective the longer I stuck with the process of building the business.

As I continued to push forward, my ability to evaluate my progress increased beyond anything I could have imagined at the beginning.

Perspective: the ability to evaluate information, situations and the like, with respect to their meaningfulness or comparative importance.

—THE LEXICON WEBSTER DICTIONARY

Richard Bach's book, Illusions: The Adventures of a Reluctant Messiah, *is one of the most motivating books I have ever read. I first read it in 1987, then again in 1988 at the recommendation of a friend who reads it every year.*

In the December, 1989, I read it for the third time. I got more out of it than I had before. I gained more insight. I was also reading parts of it that I'd never noticed.

Shortly after I finished reading it the third time, a very interesting thing happened. On January 4, 1990, I had my first lunch with Chuck Beatty. Being a little nervous, and trying to think of something brilliant to say, I told him how much I'd enjoyed reading the book. When he heard the title, he gasped, "I live my life by that book!"

It was an amazing start to an amazing relationship.

This quote from that book kept us both focused on building our business, even when it seemed that only fools would proceed.

"Argue for Your Limitations, and Sure Enough, They're Yours."

—Richard Bach

Where this quote came from is still a mystery. I've forgotten where I found it. I typed it out once, in late 1990, then put it up on the wall above my desk for motivation.

I used to read it daily—2 or 3 times on those days when the weight of what I called business ignorance *seemed too heavy to bear.*

When I look at it now, I know the truth of it.

I still have those days when it's tough to be in business. Today, though, I know I'm nurturing the supreme joy of my life.

"Do Your Work.
Not Just Your Work, but a Little More
for the Lavishing's Sake—
That Little More that is Worth All the Rest.
And if You Suffer, as You Must,
And if You Doubt, as You Must,
Do Your Work.
Put Your Heart into It and the Sky will Clear.
Then, Out of Your Very Doubt and Suffering,
Will be Born the Supreme Joy of Your Life."

—U<small>NKNOWN</small>

The National Speakers Association has been my University of Professional Speaking. It was here that I began my education in the business skills I needed to run my company. I also polished the performance skills I needed to continue to develop as a speaker. NSA professionals freely share the secrets of their success with one another, in a business where far fewer people succeed than fail.

This quote is from an article in one of my first copies of the organization's monthly magazine, **Professional Speaker***. It inspired me so much that I cut it out and taped it to my computer, where I could read it as I started each new day. As a confirmed Macintosh user, I really needed all the motivation I could muster to spend hours each day at the IBM computer I was using for my contact management software!*

"No matter what you are trying to accomplish, maintain a firm belief in your ideas, bring the greatest amount of energy to them, and be willing to endure the indignities that may result. Being a mover and a shaker in (any) profession means sticking with an idea or system longer than anyone else."

—FROM *PROFESSIONAL SPEAKER* MAGAZINE

In 1990, I met Kay Baker at a meeting of professional speakers. She impressed me as being a very positive person. She had been contributing to the the development of speakers, and the speaking industry, since 1985.

By 1991, I finally got up enough nerve to ask her to help me learn my way around this business. Before she answered my request, she asked me, "Do you want to feel good or be good?"

Fortunately, one thing I have learned is that being good involves being willing to feel bad.

Kay was my mentor in the first few years of my speaking career. I credit her with passing on more than her good attitude to me. We agree that a daily attitude check is the best way to stay in business!

"Attitude is Contagious! What are You Passing Around?"

—Kay Baker

The hardest part of being in business for myself was knowing, everyday, that most new businesses fail. Realizing how little I knew about business threatened my sense of purpose when I was tired of feeling ignorant.

A speaker once told me that the single most important marker for success in this business is having a fire in the belly. *Put another way, you must be convinced that you are on a mission—that you are an integral part of something much greater than yourself.*

This quote has helped me recognize that if I wasn't willing to risk everything, *including the possibility of failure, I would never complete my chosen mission. Once I believed that failure was an acceptable risk to take, I was able to forge ahead with less fear.*

That's when I allowed myself to care about my mission so deeply that I was willing to risk failure to succeed. Doing that gave me the courage I needed to get through the fright I experienced on a regular basis.

"Nobody Succeeds in a Big Way, Except by Risking Failure"

—William Feather

This is another quote that works well in the face of fear. It's very effective on those days when I'm half-convinced that life would be safer if I would just stand still.

Growing our business was the biggest act of creation or initiative that either one of us had ever attempted. There were so many days, during those first few years, that we were frozen still with fear. Fear that we were wrong. Fear that we'd lose everything and still not live our dreams. Fear that we'd never get in the game, much less win it.

We believed this quote. Some days, being willing to put one foot in front of the other was all we had going for us. The thought that this behavior was enough to set Providence in motion was very empowering.

"Concerning all acts of initiative and creation, there is one elementary truth, the ignorance of which kills countless good ideas and splendid plans: That the moment one definitely commits oneself, then Providence moves, too. All sorts of things occur to help one that otherwise would not have occurred."

—W. H. Murray

In the mid-80s I bought and studied The Psychology of Winning, *an audio tape program by Denis Waitley. Once I decided that* loser *no longer described me, using this tape was my first step in learning to become a winner.*

The program was excellent. I learned a great deal. In the following months, I was so involved in learning and practicing my new behaviors, I had no idea how much they had changed my life.

In 1991, I came across this quote from Denis. I was amazed at how strongly the sentiment resonated within me. I realized that I had been working so hard to overcome my liabilities that I'd forgotten about my talents and skills.

This quote remained taped to my infamous PC until the day I joyfully replaced it with a Mac. It reminds me daily to focus on all the things that I have going for me. Many of the things I thought I was NOT are the very things I've become—now that I believe they are possible.

"It's Not What You *ARE* that Holds You Back, It's What You Think You're *NOT*."

—Denis Waitley

Boris had it right! This quote from Doctor Zhivago *is one of my favorites because it validates a belief of mine.*

What's the use of getting ready if you never take the plunge? It does no good to have all the right equipment and no experience in using it. New experience has always attracted me—when I jump, I jump in with both feet. All things considered, I've had many more successes than failures. (Especially if you count learning what NOT to do as a success...)

What I love about this quote is that it reflects my belief that everything I've done so far has been "on-the-job training" for my mission in life. Whether I succeeded in each of those experiences or not, I certainly have some great stories to tell!

"(We are) Born to Live and Not to Prepare to Live."

—Boris Pasternak

Chuck and I were travelling through the 1000 Islands region of New York State when we found this poem printed in a little newspaper. We were returning home from a visit with his Canadian cousins in Clear Lake, Ontario.

The idea was exhilarating. It was a shift in perspective. I'd been feeling like I was "in over my head" in several areas of my life. The thought of being buoyant, and swimming out farther than I'd ever been before, seemed much more appealing to me than choosing to stand safely on the shore (Translate: relinquishing my dreams in fear).

That it was referred to as a "superb journey" motivated me; that I believed it could reflect my choices was pure joy!

"In the River of Life…
The soul enters the body at the river's edge
and there begins a superb journey.
Some are content to merely wade
in the shallows near the shore.
Others venture into deeper water to see
how it feels to be buoyant
and to swim."

—U̲nknown

You can never have enough motivation! This quote, like many of the quotes in this book, is interchangeable with several others: Take a step! Take a chance! Take a risk! Each thought provided an urge for my soul to continue.

There were days when it felt like I was pushing a boulder up a mountain with my nose, only to have it roll back down to the bottom again before I ever reached the top. All I could do was believe there was a purpose, even in the days and weeks when that idea seemed profoundly naive.

Beginning this business, and sticking with it, was very challenging. It still is. The inspiration I get from the thoughts of those who persevered and succeeded before me encourages me every day.

"Are You in Earnest? Seize this Very Minute!
Whatever You Can Do or Dream You Can,
Begin It.
Boldness has Genius, Power and Magic in It.
Only Engage and the Mind Grows Heated—
Begin it and the Work will be Completed."

—G̲oethe

What a great endorsement!

This is another quote from one of those books compiled solely to bring inspiring thoughts to our attention. They're so enjoyable to browse through, and I often find a keeper *like this one.*

For so many years, I was cautioned against being as enthusiastic as I naturally am. I was told that I "wasn't polite," that I "was too loud," and that I "threatened people."

How delightful to find this quote in a book of great ideas. *The more I think about it, the more enthusiastic I get!*

"Enthusiasm is the greatest asset in the world. It beats money and power and influence."

—Henry Chester

I first heard this quote from Robin Williams in the movie, "The Dead Poets Society." Carpe Diem *was the exclamation that defined his character.*

Both Chuck and I had seen this movie separately, before we met. We've seen it again several times, together. To us, the quote is a reminder to live life to the fullest, to take each day to the limit of experience. It's about understanding that being open to true love and great joy also leaves you open to great sorrow and deep pain at the same time.

Knowing we are on this road together makes the concept a joyful opportunity!

"Carpe Diem"
Seize the Day!

—Horace

Learning how to use chopsticks at the Canton House *in Poughkeepsie was one of my claims to fame in high school. I was part of the lunatic fringe. We were 17 and we were cool. Since then, I take every opportunity to eat Chinese food in Chinese restaurants wherever I go. Using chopsticks was my first attraction; now I go for something else.*

As far as I'm concerned, no matter how great the food or how sparkling the conversation, the high point of the meal is the fortune cookie for dessert. My cookie always contains a secret message to me from the Universe. That message may inspire a quiet smile, a giggle, or a sigh of relief. The nature of the message varies, but its relevance to my life is unbelievably accurate most of the time.

I keep all my fortunes together, in a wooden box that Maggie gave me years ago. Whenever I really need a boost, I open the box and take them out. After I've read them all, one by one, I always feel better.

This message arrived in a cookie in 1992, on a day when I was tired, eating alone, and a long way from home. Despite the circumstances, I laughed out loud—because, once again, it was absolutely true!

"Optimism: the cheerful frame of mind that enables the tea kettle to sing even though it's in hot water up to its nose."

—Chinese Fortune Cookie

Paying attention to, and using, all of the motivation I had collected from other people's words finally changed me from the inside out. After years of practicing what I'd learned, it was suddenly second nature for me to come up with motivational ideas of my own.

The privilege of my life has been the chance to keep…

...Spreading the Light

Part Four: (1990-1995)

This is one of my favorites, because it's exactly what I did—for years!

When I first wrote Stress Arresters *(originally* Stress Busters*), I concluded the program with this thought. It was very important to me to emphasize the idea that if the changes you are making feel* weird, *it's only because the behaviors you are trying are new for you.*

If you continue to act positively despite how it feels initially , pretty soon those new behaviors will begin to feel just like you. *And you will gain the positive results you desire.*

> "Fake It 'til You Make It!"
>
> —Maura Beatty

In 1977, it was my good fortune to be working with Gwen Nichols, a truly gifted therapist in San Diego. One of the first things she asked me to do, in the course of my therapy, was to look at myself—in the eyes!—in the bathroom mirror. I had to do it for 10 seconds every day. This was the beginning of my process of discovering that girl who was looking back at me.

Doing this got me to the next step: looking in my eyes and speaking nicely to myself. The words of this quote come from a note I had taped over my mirror for several years. I think of them as my "mental training wheels." Reading them helped me to say things to myself that I was not ready to try spontaneously.

What was so powerful about this process was that after I mastered the skill of speaking to myself in a positive way, it was so much easier to speak to others in a positive way, too. Best of all, it was not long before it was spontaneous!

"Have I
Told You Today?
You're the Greatest!"

—Maura Beatty

This was my affirmation to myself, written long before I truly believed it.

As I read the words of positive thinkers like Leo Buscaglia, Louise Hay, Rokelle Lerner, Richard Bach and others, I developed the habit of using affirmations daily. After awhile, I noticed a difference in the way I felt about myself. Soon after that, I noticed a difference in the way other people treated me. It didn't take much longer for me to start believing what I was saying.

Other people treated me better once I treated myself better. More than that, it was so much easier to be nice to people once I began to be nice to myself. It was amazing!

"Consider Yourself #1."

—Maura Beatty

This was one of the first memorable quotes from **Stress Busters.**

I have a tendency to get overwhelmed when I take on too much at once, and this tendency has resulted in a very successful pattern of procrastination. This quote reminds me that if I handle things "a bite at a time" it will reduce my habit of avoiding important tasks until the situation becomes a disaster.

It still works for me! Handling important tasks in this manner has allowed me to reduce my anxiety, frustration and guilt in situations that previously would have eaten me alive.

"No Matter How Much Pizza You're Gonna Eat, You Gotta Eat It a Bite at a Time!"

—Maura Beatty

Saying this over and over in my **Stress Arresters** *programs has increased my self confidence beyond my wildest dreams.*

This statement gets laughs in the program because I'm joking about what we want people to believe about us. The really funny part is that we usually don't believe it about ourselves.

I have been taught that our brains don't know the difference between what is real and what we imagine. It's true that I used to believe I was worthless. Much of my self confidence today is a direct result of my change in language.

> "I Do It.
> I Do It Well.
> And I Look Good
> Doin' It!"
>
> —Maura Beatty

This quote comes from one of my favorite parts of **Stress Arresters.**

Everyone laughs when I joke about "hungry nostrils" and food. As I was putting this book together, it occurred to me that being hungry—for food, love, anything—will absolutely affect your behavior.

When I was starving for love, I never stopped searching for it. When I am hungry for knowledge, I don't let anything stop me until I find what I'm looking for.

This one reminds me that hunger can absolutely direct your life—for good or not.

"Hungry Nostrils Take on a Life of Their Own"

—Maura Beatty

In 1990, I started MEA Productions. "MEA" stood for Maura Eileen Anne.

When I first began, I had no clue as to how to run a business. I did know that I believed I had a purpose. I continued to act as if I knew what I was doing, believing that somehow I would be able to pull it off.

My purpose was to share the joy I had found with other people. This affirmation was on the wall over my typewriter, and later over my Macintosh. It's still on the wall in my office—but it is more than an affirmation now. It is happening!

"Do What You Love.
Enjoy Yourself
and You Will
Bring Joy to Others."

—Maura Beatty

On an early morning flight out of Dallas, I was waiting patiently for breakfast. My 6 A.M. flight from Austin had not served anything and I was hungry! I'd heard the flight attendant mention cheese danish as a breakfast choice to a passenger in first class as I was sitting down. The thought of how good that danish was going to taste made the wait bearable.

When the flight attendant got to my seat, I piped up, "I'd like a cheese danish, please!" She looked at me in surprise and said, "We don't have any cheese danish." I looked back at her and said, "Yes, you do. I heard about it as I sat down, and it's just what I've been waiting for." Apologetically, she said, "I'm really sorry, but we don't have any cheese danish. Which would you like—pancakes or cold cereal?"

All of a sudden, I wasn't hungry. I knew somebody was getting cheese danish, and it seemed unreasonable that somebody could and I couldn't. So I said, "No, thank you" to breakfast. The flight attendant seemed amazed that I would choose nothing over something I didn't want.

She checked with me twice and got the same response. After everyone had finished eating and all the trays had been cleared away, she quietly brought me a cheese danish from first class. This quote is my reminder: never to settle for less than I want—no matter how long it takes!

"Hold Out for the Cheese Danish!"

—Maura Beatty

In 1991, I was given the opportunity to showcase at the National Speakers Association's National Convention.

I wrote a seven-minute presentation, called **Being Willing,** *especially for the showcase. I was scared out of my wits. I really needed every word I had written in the program, just to get through it!*

This is my favorite quote from what has evolved into a two-hour presentation. It reminds me of the "Industrial Strength Garlic Cape" I wear to defy the limitations of my fears.

It also reminds me of the look on George Gochenhaur's face when he saw the showcase. George has been my surrogate dad since 1975. His love got me through the scary times—before I was strong enough to write this.

"What do we need fear for anyway? Pay five bucks, see a horror movie, get scared, then get on with your life!"

—Maura Beatty

This is one of my favorite quotes of all time.

It is the last few lines of Being Willing, *and I believe, with all my heart, that this is what I am here to share.*

"What keeps you from believing that the Universe is Yours? Reach out. Embrace It. I say, 'The Sky's the Limit!' So get your bag, get your stuff, and head for the stars… I'll meet you out there."

—Maura Beatty

This quote is my formula for success. I'm following the lead of one of my heroes, Sherlock Holmes. It's elementary, my dears! The more you do it, the easier it gets.

My life's work is to share that process with other people, believing that each of us has everything we need to succeed on our own terms.

"Success Always Leaves Clues! The trick is knowing where to look for them, and then sticking with the process until you find what you seek."

—Maura Beatty

This idea came from Indiana Jones and the Last Crusade. *Remember when Indy had to make a seemingly impossible jump across a chasm to reach the Holy Grail and save his father's life? That scene is the closest representation I have ever seen of the process involved in finding your destiny. I wrote this to remind myself of what I had learned.*

In order to realize your dreams, you must first find the courage to face the obstacles—especially when they include a lack of faith in yourself and your abilities.

I believe that each one of us has been given the seeds of our own greatness, if we will only choose to do the work.

"Take Your Leap of Faith…
When You Find the Courage
to Face the Chasm
that Separates You from Your Dreams,
Then You Will See the Bridge."

—M%%AURA%% B%%EATTY%%

Epilogue

Thank you for sharing this journey with me. If you've enjoyed it, I celebrate. If it has made you think, I celebrate more.

My guess is that there are no coincidences. If you've found this book, we have something to share. All I ask is that you pass on the thoughts that mean something to you to anyone for whom it will make the difference. It's very likely that we are all a part of the process of spreading the Light in this world...

If you have any thoughts, or comments (or jokes!) you can write to us at:

>Alpha Beatty Communications
>8760-A Research Blvd., Suite 387
>Austin, Texas 78758

>Or you can reach us online at:
>MauraB624@AOL.com

Godspeed. And cool runnings!

Other Projects

Since the original publication of *Bootstrap Words*, we've completed some other projects about which you might be interested in knowing:

Our video, *Stress Arresters*, was released by South Texas Public Broadcasting in October, 1995. (Another dream come true, it's the video of that stress management program I've mentioned in this book!) If you're interested in purchasing a copy, we've enclosed an order form at the end of this book for your convenience.

In February 1996, our friends at Kendall/Hunt Publishing will release my second book, *Pizza and the Art of Life Management*. It's the companion to the *Stress Arresters* video, full of extra information to compliment the video, including worksheets and progress pages. If you are interested in purchasing a copy, we've enclosed an order form for it, as well.

If you'd like to be on our mailing list for future book releases or information about my presentations, just write us or e-mail us at the addresses on the previous page. We'd love to hear from you!

Index

A
"a Bite at a Time..." **77**
Acknowledgments *xi-xii*
Anonymous **27**

B
Bach, Richard **43**
Baker, Kay **49**
Barton, Bruce **29**
Browning, Robert **15**

C
"Cheese Danish..." **85**
Chester, Henry **63**
"Consider yourself..." **75**

D
De Chardin, Teilhard **5**
"Do it well..." **79**
"Do what you love..." **83**
"Do your work..." **45**

E
Emerson, Ralph Waldo **17**
"Enough love..." **7**

F
"Fake it 'til..." **71**
"Fear..." **87**
Feather, William **51**
France, Anatole **11**

G
Gibran, Kahlil **33, 37**
Goethe **61**

H
Horace **65**
"Hungry nostrils..." **81**

L
"Leap of faith..." **93**

M
Maggie **31**
Meyer, Paul J. **21**
Murray, W. H. **53**

O
O'Lavin, Barney **25**
"Optimism..." **67**

P
Pasternak, Boris **57**
"Perspective..." **41**
Professional Speaker Magazine **47**

R
"Reach for the stars..." **89**
Rilke, Rainier Maria **13**
"River of Life..." **59**

S
Serenity Prayer **35**
Shakespeare, William **9**
"Success..." **91**

W
Waitley, Denis **55**
Wizard of Oz, The **19**

Y
"You're the greatest..." **73**

About the Author

Maura Beatty is a professional speaker and consultant who specializes in teaching people how to communicate more positively with themselves and others. She is the president and owner of Alpha Beatty Communications.

Maura received her B.A. in Psychology from the former Corpus Christi State University (now Texas A&M University at Corpus Christi) in 1987. She is a veteran of over 11 years in the U. S. Navy.

Maura is active in the National Speakers Association and Meeting Professionals International.

She lives in Austin, Texas with her husband, Chuck, and two cats.

Order Form

Stress Arresters—*the Video!*

After seven years of presenting to audiences around the country, Maura Beatty brings her dynamic *Stress Arresters* into your home or office. This one hour video takes you on a hilarious and heart-warming trip through Maura's stress baggage. You will laugh as you learn the Four Week Plan for reducing the impact of stress in your life. Maura closes the program with her Four T's—the mental strategies for dealing with stress. Filled with warmth and humor, this program is a wonderful combination of stand-up comedy and a hug from a friend.

Pizza & the Art of Life Management

The hilarious companion volume to the *Stress Arresters* video. Complete with work pages and progress charts, this book will allow you to keep your stress under arrest long after you've begun the process. You'll refer back to these pages time and time again. This book will be released in February 1996.

Please Send Me:

_____ Copy(ies) of the "Stress Arresters" Video @ $29.95 each + Shipping

_____ Copy(ies) of "Pizza & the Art of Life Management" @ $14.95 each + Shipping

Name_____

Address_____

City_____ State _____ Zip_____ Day Phone _____

Please send $4.00 Shipping for each item ordered. Texas residents add 8% sales tax.

Mail orders to: Alpha Beatty Communications • 8760-A Research Blvd., Ste. 387 • Austin, Texas 78758